A Missed

Second

Chance

A Mosaic of Love

Beatrice Kamara Cooper

Contents

Chapter One

On My Way from School

The sun dipped low on the horizon, casting long shadows across the bustling streets as the school day came to its close. In the heart of the town, where the roads converged, there was a common meeting ground for students from disparate schools. It was here that the paths of Jason and I often crossed amid the throng of teenagers making their way homeward.

Jason, a lad of fine countenance and spirited demeanor, attended a separate academy from mine. His was an all-boys institution, while I, by contrast, belonged to a mixed school where the chatter of both boys and girls filled the halls. Yet, despite our scholastic differences, our paths intersected in that common square, where the rhythms of departure and reunion played out each afternoon.

He would be there, waiting with an air of anticipation, his gaze fixed expectantly upon the gathering crowd. For my part, I had never been one to tarry, preferring to set forth on my way towards home without delay. But Jason, it seemed, possessed a different inclination. There was a quiet constancy in his presence, a subtle insistence that we should walk together, our footsteps falling in unison upon the cobblestone streets.

We spoke of the day's lessons, the intrigues of our respective classrooms, and the fleeting moments of company shared among friends. Yet beneath the veneer of casual discourse lay an unspoken understanding, a mutual recognition of something more profound than mere acquaintance, at least on his part.

As we would cross the familiar route homeward, our words would flow effortlessly, talking about shared experiences and the budding affection that was growing inside him. I, for my part, was not oblivious to the subtle nuances of Jason's attentions. Though my heart belonged to another – a boy named Hanno, whose presence loomed large in my thoughts – I could not deny the allure of Jason's companionship. There was a warmth in his laughter, a sincerity in his gaze that spoke volumes of his regard for me.

And so we walked, two students bound by the common thread of adolescence, navigating the paths of friendship and affection. Even amid the crowd of fellow students, Jason would have eyes for me, and me only.

Beneath the surface of our growing friendship lay a delicate balance, a tension born of unspoken desires and unfulfilled expectations. Jason, it seemed, harbored hopes of winning my affection despite the knowledge that my heart belonged to another. His efforts, though earnest, were tempered by the reality of my existing attachment, a fact he could not easily ignore.

But still, he persisted, his determination undimmed by the specter of affection. Each day brought new opportunities for connection, new moments of shared laughter, and quiet understanding. And though I remained steadfast in my devotion to Hanno, I could not deny the flutter of excitement that stirred within me in Jason's presence.

Our walks home became a ritual, and so it was, in the fading light of the afternoon, that Jason and I forged a bond, a connection that would endure long after our footsteps had faded from the cobblestone streets.

Chapter Two

Attending Church Practice

As I began attending our local church, it was merely a routine affair, nothing extraordinary. But then, like a refreshing breeze on a hot summer day, Hanno entered the scene. Every girl's head turned when he walked in—impeccably groomed, exuding confidence, with a smile that could brighten even the gloomiest of days. I couldn't help but notice the small details: his perfectly shined shoes, his well-mannered speech that demanded attention, and those teeth—straight as an arrow, gleaming like pearls in the sunlight.

But despite his undeniable charm, I knew better than to let myself get swept away. Girls like me didn't chase after boys, no matter how intriguing they seemed. So, I kept my distance, observing from afar as he seamlessly integrated into our church community.

It was during one of the youth meetings that I first truly noticed him. As the announcement for the next gathering echoed through the hall, I caught his eye, and the next thing I knew, he was there, taking a seat beside me with that disarming smile of his. My heart fluttered, but I maintained my composure, returning his greeting with a shy smile of my own.

From that moment on, our paths seemed to intertwine more and more. Whether it was the casual chats before meetings or the shared moments of camaraderie, I found myself drawn to him in ways I couldn't fully understand. And then came that fateful day when he sat so close to me that our hips touched—a simple gesture that sent my heart into a frenzy.

As we exchanged pleasantries, I couldn't help but feel a sense of anticipation tingling in the air. His presence was electrifying, and for a brief moment, I allowed myself to entertain the possibility of something more. But as quickly as it had come, the moment passed, and we found ourselves once again parting ways, each retreating to our respective corners of homes.

Yet, despite the brevity of our interactions, the memory of that encounter lingered like a sweet melody, replaying in my mind like a cherished song. And as I made my way home that evening, I couldn't shake the feeling that perhaps, just perhaps, there was something special waiting to unfold between us.

In the midst of our usual youth meeting, Hanno and I had settled comfortably into the role of friends— nothing more, or so I thought. Yet, on this particular evening, there was a subtle shift in the air, a tension that belied our casual camaraderie.

"Beatrice," Hanno's voice broke through the chatter, drawing my attention. With a nod, I acknowledged him, unaware of the bombshell he was about to drop.

"There's someone in our group that I've been thinking a lot about," he confessed, his words hanging heavy between us.

My heart sank as the realization dawned on me. Though I tried to hide my disappointment behind a practiced smile, inside, I felt a wave of heartbreak wash over me. But I couldn't let Hanno see how his words had affected me. Instead, I mustered up the courage to play along, offering to help him navigate his feelings for this mystery girl.

Little did I know, the girl he spoke of was none other than myself. It wasn't until weeks later, on a night that would become etched in my memory, that Hanno revealed the truth.

It was a balmy evening, the kind that beckons you outdoors, where laughter mingles with the faint strains of music in the air. As I stood outside my home, enveloped in the pulsating rhythm of the night, Hanno appeared before me like a vision.

With a gentle touch, he drew me close, our eyes locking in a silent exchange that spoke volumes. And then, in a moment that felt suspended in time, he uttered those words that would change everything: "Do you remember when I told you about a girl I'm interested in? That girl is you."

Time seemed to stand still as I processed his confession, the world around us fading into insignificance. And with a smile that mirrored my own, I accepted his proposition, our hands intertwining as we ventured into the night together, a new chapter unfolding before us.

In the euphoria of our newfound connection, Hanno couldn't contain his excitement. It was as if the entire world needed to know that I had accepted him as my boyfriend. Leading me to the entrance of the bustling community center, he gestured for me to take a seat on his lap—a gesture that caught me off guard yet somehow felt strangely comforting.

As I settled onto his lap, the warmth of his embrace enveloping me, Hanno embarked on a mission to introduce me to everyone who crossed our path. With each handshake and smile, he made it abundantly clear that I was now an integral part of his life—a fact he wanted to broadcast to the world.

But as the night wore on and the festivities began to wind down, it was time for me to return home. Reluctantly, Hanno released me from his grasp, promising to return the next day—a promise he kept without fail.

Excitedly, I shared the news of our blossoming relationship with my sister, who, like everyone else, couldn't help but be swept away by Hanno's charm. He was smart, handsome, and tall—a perfect match for a young girl like myself. And so, our routine of seeing each other every Tuesday and Thursday continued, our walks home from church becoming cherished moments of togetherness.

Whether it was him following me to my area or me trailing behind him, our post-church rendezvous became a cherished tradition—a chance to bask in each other's company and reaffirm our bond. As the weeks turned into months, it seemed as though everyone in the church knew of our relationship—a testament to the ease and joy with which we navigated our young love. I still clung to the memory of that magical evening the promise of many more wonderful memories to come.

Chapter Three

Falling In Love for The First Time

As Hanno and I strolled from the bustling community center, there was an enchanting ease to the way he held my hand – a delicate balance of firmness and gentleness that sent a wave of comfort through me, even in the cool night air. Our steps synced effortlessly as we made our way toward my house, a silent understanding weaving between us like a secret language only we could decipher. Lost in the haze of my thoughts, I couldn't help but marvel at the sight of him beside me, a perfect match in height and demeanor, a vision I couldn't tear my eyes away from.

But the calmness of our walk was inevitably interrupted as we neared my home, the looming presence of parental rules casting a shadow over our stolen moments together. Like most parents, mine had strict instructions about boys – "None allowed," they'd warn. And so, there we stood, on the precipice of my doorstep, our silent bubble threatening to burst.

Hanno halted our progress, prompting me to do the same, his hands gently cradling my face as he positioned himself before me. In the dim light, his features were still clear to me, his eyes a captivating constellation in the darkness. With a tenderness that enveloped me like a warm blanket, he drew me closer, not for a kiss but for an embrace so sweet and comforting it felt like home. His presence enveloped me, his breath a gentle whisper against my temple, his heartbeat a rhythmic melody that echoed in my ears. And amidst it all, the scent of his cologne lingered, mingling with the night air in a symphony of senses.

In a fleeting moment, he pulled me even closer, as if there could never be enough space between us, his arms wrapping around me with a warmth that seeped into my bones. And then, his whispered words brushed against my ear, soft and sincere — "I'll miss you." A smile tugged at my lips, a flutter of butterflies dancing in my stomach as I basked in the warmth of his affection.

But as the night whispered its inevitable goodbye, we reluctantly began to disentangle ourselves, the start of our embrace mirrored in its end. His hands lingered on my cheeks, his gaze unwavering as he spoke, a moment tinged with the awkwardness of young love blossoming for the first time. And as I stood there, enraptured by the sound of his voice, he promised to return tomorrow, a smile lighting up his face in confirmation. With a flutter of excitement in my chest, I nodded in agreement, turning slowly to make my way home.

Though the sound of my own footsteps echoed in the quiet night, I couldn't resist stealing a glance over my shoulder. And there he stood, a solitary figure bathed in moonlight, his gaze fixed on me with an intensity that sent shivers down my spine. With a wave of goodbye, I turned my gaze forward, the memory of his lingering presence guiding me home, a promise of tomorrow's rendezvous tucked safely in my heart.

As I stood on the threshold of my home, the warm glow of the porch light spilling out around me, my grandmother greeted me with a curious tilt of her head, her eyes catching the gleam of happiness reflected in my own. "What's got you smiling like the sun?" she inquired, her voice laced with gentle curiosity. With a practiced ease, I replied, "Oh, nothing, granny," a white lie slipping easily from my lips as I sidestepped her questioning gaze, the grin on my face too infectious to contain.

Slipping into the familiarity of my bedroom, the weight of the day finally settling around me like a cozy blanket, I couldn't shake the feeling of warmth that lingered in my chest, a reminder of the special connection I shared with Hanno. As I drifted into sleep, it felt as though I lay upon clouds, the memory of his tender embrace cradling me in a sense of belonging that transcended the confines of my ordinary bed.

But with the dawn of a new day came the agonizing crawl of time, each passing hour stretching out before me like an eternity as I awaited the promised reunion with Hanno. Though doubt crept in, I dared to hope, my heart fluttering with the anticipation of his arrival. Yet, as the appointed hour drew near, a wave of disappointment threatened to engulf me, and the weight of uncertainty pressed heavily upon my shoulders.

And then, just when it seemed all hope was lost, his voice cut through the air, calling out my name in a soft, melodic tone that set my heart racing. "Beatrice," he called, and at that moment, I knew — he had come for me. With a joy that bubbled up from deep within, I turned to face him, my eyes alight with excitement as I beheld his familiar form, his smile a warmth against the fading daylight.

With a few quick strides, we closed the distance between us, our smiles mirroring one another as we embraced beneath the soft hues of the setting sun. Unable to retreat to the safety of my home, we found comfort in the bustling energy of the community center's outdoor seating area, the world around us alive with the hum of conversation and the gentle murmur of passing lovers.

As the evening unfolded, we lost ourselves in each other's company, our conversation flowing effortlessly like a river winding its way through the landscape of our shared experiences. Friends drifted in and out of our orbit, their presence only adding to the magic of the moment as we reveled in the simple pleasure of being together. And amidst it all, there were those stolen glances, those fleeting moments of connection that spoke volumes without the need for words.

In that no-stress atmosphere, surrounded by the warmness of his presence and the gentle hum of life around us, I couldn't help but feel as though I were floating on air, suspended in a bubble of bliss that seemed to stretch on for eternity. And as the night wore on and the stars began to twinkle overhead, I knew that in his arms, I had found my heaven, my refuge from the chaos of the world outside.

Hanno and I continued our precious moments among the hustle and bustle of our schedules, stealing away hand in hand not only before but also after our youth practices, which convened faithfully every Tuesday and Thursday. Oh, the sweetness of those memories, like whispers of a cherished melody lingering in the air.

Yet, in the laughter and embraces, there came a day when our carefree stroll home took an unexpected turn. Unbeknownst to me, as I stood outside my house, lost in the warmth of Hanno's presence, my favorite uncle, Uncle Foday Dumbuya, caught sight of us. Little did I know the storm that awaited me at home.

As Hanno bid me farewell, his departure heralding the end of another evening filled with shared laughter and stolen moments, I made my way toward my house, oblivious to the storm brewing just beyond its threshold. But as I stepped onto the familiar path leading to my front door, the serenity of the night shattered like glass, replaced by the sharp sting of a slap that echoed through the darkness.

For a moment, silence enveloped us both; the weight of my uncle's disapproval hung heavy in the air. And then, like a sudden downpour, his words came crashing down upon me, a torrent of questions and accusations that left me reeling in their wake. With a heavy heart, I retreated into the safety of my room, the echoes of his anger still ringing in my ears.

Yet, with the dawn of a new day came a glimmer of remorse as my uncle sought me out to express his concerns and fears, his voice softened by the light of morning. With a humility that touched my heart, he implored me to be cautious and responsible, his apology a balm to the wounds of the previous night's altercation.

And in that moment, I found it in my heart to forgive him, understanding the depth of his love and concern for me.

When I shared the incident with Hanno, his reaction was one of stunned silence, his usually animated demeanor subdued by the weight of my uncle's disapproval. And though our walk home that day was shrouded in an uncomfortable silence, the bond between us remained unbroken, a testament to the strength of our connection.

In time, the storm clouds of misunderstanding cleared, and we resumed our rendezvous with a newfound sense of caution and discretion, our love blossoming amidst the challenges that life threw our way. And as we walked hand in hand into the sunset, I knew that together, we could weather any storm that came our way.

Chapter Four

Crisis

As the sun rose and set, marking the passage of time with its golden hues, Hanno and I found ourselves swept up in a whirlwind of connection that seemed to defy the ordinary laws of friendship. Our bond transcended the casual conversations of everyday life, weaving us together in a kind of love that only seemed to grow stronger with each passing day.

Communication became our lifeline, threading through our days with the delicate touch of whispered secrets and shared dreams. Whether face-to-face or carried by the whispers of mutual friends, our words danced between us like notes in a symphony of affection. Hanno had a way with words that was nothing short of enchanting, and each message was like a masterpiece painted with the brushstrokes of his love.

Sometimes, his notes were simple reminders of our bond, small tokens of affection that brightened even the dreariest of days. Other times, they explored deeper waters, diving into the depths of our hearts to discover the complexities of our emotions. We were a team united in our shared vision of a future filled with promise and possibility.

I remember one evening as we wandered through a neighborhood bathed in the soft glow of streetlights and the occasional twinkle of a distant star. The contrast of bright and dim seemed to mirror the complexities of our own relationship, a patchwork of light and shadow that danced around us as we walked hand in hand.

Suddenly, Hanno stopped in his tracks, his gaze fixed on a house illuminated against the gathering darkness. It stood tall and proud, a display of prosperity in a sea of suburban sameness. With a tender touch, he turned me to face it, his eyes alight with a vision of our future together.

"Someday," he said, his voice soft but sure, "We'll have a home like that. A place where our love can flourish, where our dreams can take root and grow."

I couldn't help but smile at his words, warmed by the thought of the life we could build together. But then, his tone shifted, a note of vulnerability creeping into his voice as he whispered, "Please don't let someone take you away from me."

Confusion flickered in my mind, uncertainty casting shadows across our shared moment. But before I could voice my questions, he took my hand once more, and we resumed our journey with renewed purpose and love that burned brighter than any streetlight in the night.

As we meandered through the streets, stealing kisses in the shadowy corners that seemed to hold a certain enchantment, I found myself utterly captivated by the warmth of Hanno's embrace. His touch was like a lifeline, grounding me in a world that felt both exhilarating and comforting all at once. Eventually, our footsteps led us to my doorstep, where we exchanged a tender goodnight kiss before parting ways for the evening.

Our time together had become a natural rhythm, an expected cadence of our lives. Hanno and I were no longer just individuals; we had become a unit, a singular entity, or so I thought.

While I remained dedicated to my studies, excelling in my academic pursuits and proudly wearing the badge of a prefect—a position of honor bestowed upon students who demonstrated exceptional academic achievement and exemplary behavior—my world was about to be rocked by an unexpected revelation.

One day, a fellow student—a non-prefect—approached me with a startling confession. She claimed that Hanno harbored deep feelings for me, professing his love and even declaring me as the girl he intended to marry. However, her tale took a sad turn when she revealed that despite his proclamations of affection for me, he had been with her intimately the previous night.

Time seemed to stand still as I grappled with the weight of her words. The shock and disbelief threatened to engulf me as I struggled to comprehend the betrayal unfolding before me. I wanted to dismiss her claims as mere gossip, a malicious attempt to sow discord in our relationship. But the nagging doubt lingered, gnawing at the edges of my mind like a persistent ache.

Unable to focus on my studies in the wake of this revelation, I found myself consumed by troubling emotions—pain, confusion, and a profound sense of betrayal. I needed answers and clarity amidst the confusion that threatened to swamp me.

With determination coursing through my veins, I set out to confront Hanno, to demand the truth and reclaim the shattered pieces of my heart. But as I embarked on this quest for closure, I couldn't shake the sense of anger and resentment bubbling within me.

I was practically sprinting to see him; my mind was filled with questions and uncertainties, clamoring for answers. But fate seemed determined to test me that day, as it coincided with our church practice. Hanno must have sensed my inner turmoil, his brow furrowing with concern as he tried to read the storm brewing behind my eyes. I couldn't bring myself to broach the subject before practice, so I bided my time, waiting for the inevitable confrontation to take place.

As we made our way home after the final chords of the choir had faded into the evening air, the weight of our impending conversation hung heavy in the air. I couldn't bear to prolong the agony any longer, so as soon as we stepped outside the church, I mustered the courage to confront him.

"We need to talk," I said, my voice betraying the turmoil raging within me. Hanno's expression shifted, a flicker of uncertainty crossing his features as he braced himself for whatever was to come. With a deep breath, I plunged into the heart of the matter, recounting the damning tale that had been told to me.

He stood there, his gaze shifting away as if searching for the right words to soothe the situation. But try as he might, explanations eluded him, leaving an uncomfortable silence in their wake. And then, with a heavy sigh, he uttered those words that would change everything.

"I don't want you to believe her."

It wasn't a denial, not really. More like a feeble attempt to deflect the truth, to shield me from the painful reality staring us both in the face. But his words landed like a blow to the chest, shattering the fragile illusion of trust that had once bound us together.

At that moment, the distance between us grew immeasurable, a gaping abyss of doubt and betrayal stretching out before me. The silence that followed spoke volumes, a somber acknowledgment that our relationship would never be the same again.

Oh, how I wished for the simplicity of the day before when our love was untainted by suspicion and deceit. But life has a cruel way of shattering our illusions, leaving us to pick up the pieces of our shattered hearts and forge ahead into an uncertain future.

Chapter Five

Loved By Two Boys

Remember that feeling of walking in the sunshine? Like every song was your anthem, and your heart vibrated with a love so epic it belonged in a coming-of-age novel? That was me until it wasn't. Kaput. Like a perfectly built sandcastle stomped flat by a rogue toddler. Why? Why would he trade something so real for...well, whatever shiny thing caught his eye? The questions echoed in my head like a broken record.

Heartbreak can be a good motivator though, at least it was for me. I used to dream of making a difference, not just for myself but for the people who mattered. Now, that dream became a laser focus. I crammed textbooks harder than ever, determined to ace my classes and prove I wasn't defined by some jerk with roving affections.

One day, there he was. Jason. The walking laugh track, the master of distraction. Now, whether he knew about the Hanno-shaped hole in my heart, who knows?

Gossip travels faster than light in our teenyverse. But he didn't bring it up. Maybe he sensed the wreckage zone around me. Jason was a good friend, the kind who could shove your worries aside with a goofy joke. Exactly what I needed, along with therapy sessions and a gallon of ice cream (not necessarily in that order).

There was this other guy, Hanno. The one who'd ripped my heart out. Seeing him again was a confusing mess. A part of me wanted to take him back and rewrite the ending. But forgiveness? Major struggle bus. I'd dissect the situation in my head, each replay making me angrier. How could you say you love someone and then do that? It's a mystery that would rival the Bermuda Triangle.

So there I was, stuck between a confusing past and an unsure future. But hey, at least I was surrounded by good friends, good grades, and the burning desire to prove that I was more than just a heartbreak statistic.

So, life lurched on. Church choir practice, like clockwork. And there he was, Hanno, trying to navigate the wreckage zone he'd built for us. It felt like a slow-motion train crash of a relationship – a tragic end we both probably saw coming a mile away. It was like watching a plant wilt, helpless and inevitable. He wasn't the same person to me anymore, no matter how hard he tried to rewind. The crazy thing? I'd poured my whole heart into him, and it still wasn't enough. There was nothing left to salvage.

We both floundered, desperate for answers. Talks devolved into a loop of apologies, justifications, and empty promises that clanged hollow in the space between us. The damage was done, a permanent marker stain on the perfect picture we once had. I was a walking sadness manifesto, while Hanno ping-ponged between desperation and frustration. Then, to twist the knife a little further, he… well, let's just say he didn't exactly help.

But hey, life isn't all breakups and bad decisions. National Exams were looming – the Everest of high school, the gateway drug to college applications. Getting a stellar score was the only way to snag a spot at a decent uni. Forget boys, forget heartbreak – this was a fight for my future. So, I channeled all that leftover emotional energy into laser focus. Textbooks became my new best friends; cramming became my new superpower. Studying became my war cry – a battle cry against heartbreak and a fight for a future that wouldn't be defined by the ashes of this relationship.

Every highlighter stroke, every memorized equation, was a brick laid on the foundation of my new reality. The library became my sanctuary, the hum of fluorescent lights and the frantic scribbling of classmates a strange kind of white noise that drowned out the deafening silence of the breakup. It wasn't easy. There were late nights fueled by lukewarm coffee and tear-stained notes. But with every passing day, the focus on my future grew sharper, pushing the ache in my heart further down. It wasn't about forgetting Hanno, not entirely. It was about proving to myself, and maybe even the universe, that I was more than just a casualty of a failed relationship. This was my chance to rewrite the narrative, to trade heartbreak for a future brimming with possibility.

So, I was just dodging heartbreak bullets from Hanno while cramming for the National Exams – talk about pressure! But that wasn't all the drama swirling in my life. Back at my uncle's place, things were…hellish. If

I haven't mentioned it already, I moved in with him after Dad left for his ministry gig across the country. Big mistake. Turns out, his common-law wife — nothing less of a witch, because that woman was pure evil — made Cruella de Vil look like Mary Poppins. Turning off the lights while I studied? Just the tip of the iceberg. She was the reason most of my childhood memories came with a side of emotional scarring. Everyone else loved us, but her? She loathed us with the fiery passion of a thousand suns.

Needing an escape hatch faster than you can say, "toxic environment," I peaced out and moved in with a distant relative. Finally, some peace and quiet to focus on those all-important exams. I'd visit my uncle and siblings occasionally, but one visit became the ultimate "hold my juice box" moment. Picture this: I'm walking home when I hear this EXPLOSION of yelling coming from my uncle's place. Now, I was no stranger to drama, but this sounded like a Shakespearean tragedy in full swing.

I barged in, ready to face a rabid raccoon or a rogue blender gone haywire, only to find…my sister smack dab in the middle of a screaming match with her best friend.

Total... drama. Turns out, the best friend in question was also getting a little…friendly with Hanno. Like, seriously, Hanno? You betrayed not just me, but my freaking SISTER? The girl who was practically an extension of our family? My jaw hit the floor faster than a dropped textbook. This wasn't heartbreak anymore; this was a full-on emotional cluster bomb. Just when I thought things couldn't get any worse, Hanno proved me spectacularly wrong.

Back at my temporary digs with a distant relative, I dove headfirst into studying. Exams were looming, and education suddenly felt like my life raft in this chaotic sea.

Here's the thing about Jason, though. Even after I moved, he kept showing up. Not in a creepy way, mind you, more like a goofy ray of sunshine in my storm clouds. We still weren't a "thing," but he knew how to make me laugh, even if it was just for a stolen moment. A much-needed escape from the emotional wreckage Hanno left behind.

Speaking of wreckage, I never confronted Hanno about the whole "sister's best friend" debacle. It felt pointless. There's a certain…bro code…you just don't mess with your girlfriend's quasi-sister. Apparently, he and the friend flamed out fast and furious. But guess who swooped in as his knight in shining armor? My own sister! The one who just went nuclear on her ex-bestie. Me? I was radio silent to Hanno. He could use my sister as his messenger pigeon all he wanted, but I wasn't budging.

Finally, exams arrived, and then…vanished. Freedom! I packed my bags and headed back to the house – back to my uncle, siblings, and the ever-present Maleficent (seriously, that nickname was sticking).

One evening, after a visit with Jason (innocent, maybe a stolen kiss or two, but definitely no horizontal mambo), I was walking home. It was dark, and there, perched on the fence by the community center, was my sister. And who was next to her but Hanno?

Ugh. My stomach did a somersault. Technically, I was free to do whatever I wanted. But let's just say witnessing that little reunion wasn't exactly on my "fun things to see" list. Part of me wanted to run a mile in the opposite direction.

The next thing I remember was bolting through the front door, my heart hammering a frantic rhythm against my ribs. Then – bam! Jason grabbed my hand. Hanno shot up from the fence like a startled jackrabbit, heading straight for us. My sister's voice cracked with tension, demanding Jason let go. It was total meltdown mode.

Confused and scared, I yanked my hand free with the strength of ten angry rhinos. I sprinted towards the house, legs pumping like pistons, every step fueled by pure fight-or-flight panic. I practically flung myself through the door, slamming it shut with a resounding boom. Finally, blessed silence. For now, at least.

This whole love triangle thing? It had been uncharted territory. I'd never been there, never wanted to go. Two guys vying for my attention – an ego boost in theory, but right now? It had been pure torture. Hanno had shattered my heart with his…well, let's just say his loyalty skills needed a serious upgrade. Jason, on the other hand, had been a ray of sunshine in this emotional hurricane. But here's the kicker: my family couldn't stand him.

Accusations had flown faster than spitballs. My uncle's baby mama (seriously, that nickname was gold) had claimed Jason wouldn't marry me because of some clan nonsense that felt straight out of Romeo and Juliet. My sister, bless her heart, had thought he was "too dark," a comment that left a bitter taste in my mouth. Meanwhile, everyone adored Hanno – except me, of course. I had been stuck between a rock and a confusingly charming place.

I couldn't go back to Hanno, not after the heartbreak and humiliation. The thought of him made my stomach churn like a washing machine on a spin cycle. Jason's affection had been undeniable, but the family drama felt like quicksand, threatening to swallow me whole. He kept saying he loved me, his words earnest and sweet, but my brain had been fried from the emotional rollercoaster. Every time I looked at him, I saw a potential future filled with whispered disapproval and disapproving stares.

So, I did what any sensible (questionable?) teenager would have done: I punted. I gave up on both of them. Sure, other guys circled, vying for my attention. But none of them compared to the love I'd lost for Hanno, a love that now felt laced with a bitter aftertaste, and the confusing fondness I felt for Jason. This whole mess had been a recipe for disaster, and I was the main ingredient. But hey, at least the door was locked. For now.

The silence, however, had been a fragile thing. I knew, with a bone-deep certainty, that this wouldn't be the last act of this drama. Hanno wouldn't give up easily, not with his pride bruised. Jason, bless his persistent heart, wouldn't disappear either. And my family? Well, let's just say their opinions were about as welcome as a skunk at a picnic.

As I lay in bed that night, the shadows on my wall morphing into menacing shapes, I realized something terrifying. There were no easy answers here. No clear path forward. Just a tangled mess of emotions, conflicting loyalties, and the very real possibility that things were about to get a whole lot worse before they got better.

Chapter Six

Getting Married to Another

During this wild chapter of my life, I was stuck in the limbo of waiting for my exam scores from the Department of Education. All the while, I was caught in this weird triangle of attention from both Hanno and Jason. Honestly, it was hard not to notice or be affected by it. But, I knew I had to stay focused on the bigger picture: getting into university and, more specifically, medical school.

Amid all the chaos, there were still moments that stood out—moments that were fun or just plain unforgettable. Like the way, Hanno and Jason, and even their families, seemed to be orbiting around me. Jason's Aunt Paulla, for example, was the absolute best. She wasn't just nice; she had this amazing smile that could light up a room. She had perfectly aligned teeth and these bright, friendly eyes. Every time I visited Jason, she made me feel so welcome and at ease. She turned what could have been awkward visits into something I actually looked forward to.

Then, everything changed. Like, massively. That night started off like any other. I went to bed, totally unaware of what was about to go down. In the middle of the night, I was jolted awake by these loud noises. At first, I thought they were fireworks, but they were way too close for that. Confusion set in as I tried to make sense of the chaos around me.

We were under attack. Rebels had stormed the city, overthrown the government, and taken control. This wasn't some distant news story—it was happening right outside my bedroom. I was paralyzed with shock and fear, lying there until the first light of dawn.

By then, the rebels had left our compound, but not without leaving a chilling promise: they would return. This was the new reality. My safe, predictable life was turned upside down in one night. And as the sun rose, I knew nothing would ever be the same again.

Chaos reigned everywhere. People were running back and forth, uncertain and afraid. I stood there, just as confused, knowing I had to make a decision fast. Finally, I resolved to leave the country. My siblings and some relatives gathered at my place, and when I told them my plan, everyone agreed—except my dad. He was adamant that we should stay, believing the Lord would protect us. After some convincing, he reluctantly agreed to go.

We headed to a place where we hoped to find a boat since the roads were too dangerous for cars. The area was packed with people, all desperate to escape, and not enough boats to go around. Miraculously, we managed to secure one. We hurriedly loaded our few belongings and then ourselves onto the boat.

As we sailed away, the skyline of the city—those once tall, proud buildings—faded into the distance. I felt a mix of relief and helplessness, watching my home disappear. But the danger wasn't over. Warplanes roared above us, dropping bombs on other boats, targeting what they thought were threats. It felt like a miracle that we were spared. Why did we make it out alive? I can't say for sure, except that it felt like divine protection.

At that moment, our future was uncertain, but we had survived the night. And sometimes, survival is enough to give you hope for another day.

Our escape was anything but smooth sailing. First, we discovered the gas we had bought was contaminated with water, which left us scrambling to find the right fuel for the boat. Then, we found ourselves stuck on a sandbar, a literal pile of sand in the middle of the deep blue sea. It was dangerous and terrifying, but somehow, we managed to overcome both hurdles and kept moving forward.

After two tense days at sea, we finally reached the seaport of Guinea, a neighboring country. The port workers there looked at us like we were some kind of miracle. They couldn't believe such a small boat had traveled so far with so many people on board. They concluded that divine intervention must have been at play and treated us with an almost reverent caution.

This worked out well for us—they upgraded our lodging, fed us, and even called the local UN office. The UN representatives arrived with a vehicle and took us to a refugee camp. We were now officially refugees—safe from immediate danger but in a place that felt far from home.

Life at the camp was strange and unsettling. One particular UN subcontractor, Jal, couldn't seem to stay away from me. I was in no mood for romantic entanglements, given my already complicated feelings involving Hanno and Jason. But Jal was persistent, showing up far too often to be just a coincidence. Eventually, it became clear that his frequent visits were to see me. Despite the unresolved emotions I had for Hanno and Jason, Jal's persistence started to wear down my defenses.

My dad took an immediate liking to Jal. In fact, he spoke highly of him even before the rest of the family got to know him. Dad's approval made it harder to dismiss Jal entirely. So, despite the chaotic backdrop of our lives, Jal managed to carve out a place in my heart, setting the stage for a relationship that I hadn't anticipated. In this confusing mix of survival, fear, and unexpected connections, I found myself navigating not just the external chaos but the internal turmoil of love and loyalty.

As life would have it, my relationship with Jal turned into something profound and unexpected. Jal was this striking figure—nearly six feet tall, with a voice that could command a room and a presence that was hard to ignore. From the moment we met, his attention was unwavering. Despite my complicated love situation, which I tried to explain to him, he never wavered. In fact, his persistence made me start to see him as a way to finally choose between Jason and Hanno. Slowly but surely, his determination melted my resistance, and before I knew it, I was falling for him.

Eventually, Jal did the classic romantic move: he asked my dad for my hand in marriage. When he proposed, I said yes, thinking this would finally resolve my tangled feelings. We got married, and for a moment, everything seemed perfect. But reality has a way of complicating things.

Despite our new life together, the shadows of Hanno and Jason never really disappeared. Jal became convinced that one of them would swoop in and take me away like I was some sort of trophy. This constant fear gnawed at our marriage, creating tensions that were hard to overcome.

Yet, out of this complex and often turbulent relationship came two amazing daughters. Mary Cooper, who walked across the stage at the University of Fredonia on May 18th, 2024, clutching her degree in Marketing, and Agnes Cooper, who is gearing up to start her adventure at The University of Ohio this fall. They are our pride and joy, our testament to the good that came from our union.

But despite these beautiful moments, our marriage couldn't withstand the unresolved issues that plagued it. In 2010, Jal and I decided to part ways, marking the end of one chapter and the beginning of another. It was a painful transition, but it was also a chance to redefine my life and find a new path forward.

Chapter Seven

Being a Single Parent

Even though I found myself in a distant land, Guinea, with Jal's charming attention lavished upon me—a welcome distraction, I must admit—my thoughts often drifted back to Hanno. Before Jal swept me off my feet with his unwavering affection, I had secretly hoped that Hanno would come searching for me, that he would realize his mistake and seek me out. But alas, that fantasy remained just that—a fantasy.

Imagine my shock when I learned that Hanno had actually set foot in the very country where I now resided, not with the intention of finding me or even inquiring about my well-being, but solely for the purpose of shopping. Shopping! The audacity of it all left me dumbfounded. He was mere miles away from my doorstep, yet he couldn't spare a moment to check in on me. It felt like a slap in the face, an insult to the years we had spent together. How could someone be so callous, so utterly oblivious to the pain they inflict?

In stark contrast, Jal's steadfast devotion only served to highlight Hanno's shortcomings. Jal, with his rugged masculinity and warm, resonant voice that gave me butterflies, was a breath of fresh air in a world tainted by disappointment. He knew all about my complicated history with both Hanno and Jason, yet he never let it deter him. If anything, it seemed to fuel his determination to win my heart.

I'll admit, Jal was quite the catch—standing tall at almost six feet, with a presence that commanded attention and a sense of humor that never failed to leave me in stitches. His proposal came like a whirlwind; he couldn't wait to put a ring on it. Was it too hasty a decision? Perhaps. But in a world plagued by uncertainty and unrest, sometimes you have to seize happiness wherever you find it.

With rebels wreaking havoc in the region, I couldn't afford to wait around for a love that may never come to fruition. Jal offered stability, security, and, most importantly, love. So, I took a leap of faith, saying yes to forever with a man who promised to be my rock in a stormy sea. And you know what? It was the best decision

I ever made. Despite the chaos raging outside, within the walls of our home, I found solace and contentment. And as I walked down the aisle to become his wife, I knew deep in my heart that I was exactly where I was meant to be.

When I heard that Hanno and his family had a full-on crying session after they found out I got married, I was like, "What did they expect me to do? Just sit around and wait forever?" Not a chance. Jal turned out to be an amazing husband. He provided for us and gave me all the attention and love I could ever want. The guy wouldn't even let me cook, which is a pretty big deal for an African wife. Jal was truly great.

I remember when I couldn't conceive after almost three years of marriage. It was tough, a situation where some men might give up on their wives. But not Jal. He stood by me, never making me feel less than. Maybe it helped that he already had two kids, a girl and a boy, from before we met. But still, Jal was a rock.

So, maybe it seemed like I was the one with the problem. You could assume that, right? But no, it wasn't really that simple. I chalked it up to God's timing. Jal and I decided to seek medical help, bouncing from one doctor to another, trying to figure out what was wrong. And guess what? They all said we were fine.

Then, one doctor's words hit me like a light bulb moment. He told me to remember that children are a gift from God, and they'd come at the right time. That was the last doctor we visited because I realized he was right. Only God can bless us with babies, and He's never late, even if we don't always get that.

Jal, being his amazing self, said, "If you still want to visit another doctor, we can." But I decided it was time to stop. I told Jal I'd do one last thing: fast and pray. After that, I'd just wait on the Lord. So, I did. I took three days and fasted—a dry fast, no food, no water.

On the third and final day of my fast, something extraordinary happened. I was close to breaking my fast when three pastors from our church showed up at our home completely unannounced. They seemed as surprised as I was, not really sure why they felt compelled to visit. One of them said, "I don't know what you were praying for, but whatever it is, the Lord has answered your prayers." The joy I felt was indescribable, probably similar to what Mary felt when the angel told her she was going to give birth to Jesus. They prayed for me and our home, and then they left as suddenly as they had arrived. It felt magical, almost spiritual.

A couple of months later, I found out I was pregnant! Pregnant! It was the most joyful moment ever. We had a beautiful baby girl named Mary Dawusu Cooper— "Mary" after my mother, "Dawusu" after her paternal grandmother, and "Cooper," of course, after her father.

Four years later, we were blessed with another daughter. We named her Agnes Jaltrice Cooper. Notice how her middle name is a blend of "Jal" from her dad and "trice" from my name, Beatrice? These girls are such blessings, bringing joy to everyone they meet.

Our story had its ups and downs, but it led to these incredible moments and two beautiful daughters. They are living reminders that sometimes, you just have to trust in the timing and keep the faith.

But then, everything fell apart. Jal started acting out, and to say he was having a midlife crisis would be an understatement. He turned into someone I barely recognized—a guy I would have once called loving and affectionate was now a complete stranger. "What's happening to you?" I would ask, desperate for an answer. "Please, don't ruin our family," I would plead, but it was like he couldn't hear me. The frustration was unbearable, and the helplessness even worse.

Jal and I stopped entirely understanding each other. Our once-happy home felt like it was crumbling around us. Conversations turned into fights, and all the efforts from our friends and family to help us patch things up fell flat. I felt like I was losing my grip on reality. Maybe I did, who knows? All I knew was that we were no longer the people we used to be.

It got so bad that we became like cats and dogs, constantly at each other's throats. We separated a few times, but each time, it felt more and more like the end. I couldn't keep living in this toxic cycle, especially with the kids caught in the middle. So, I made the hardest decision of my life. I moved out, got an apartment, and eventually filed for divorce.

Jal begged me to reconsider. He said he was ready to fix things, and for a moment, with enough convincing from him and our friends and family, I thought maybe we could try again. But it didn't work. No matter how hard we tried, we couldn't get back to what we once had. So, I stood my ground. I refused to drag out the separation any longer. No more apologies, no more second chances.

And so, we divorced. It was an incredibly painful process, especially with the kids involved. But in the end, it was the only way to find some peace and move forward.

We tried to make sure the girls were affected as little as possible by the divorce. I wanted them to have easy access to their dad whenever they needed, so I rented an apartment within walking distance of his place. This way, if he couldn't come to pick them up, it would be simple for me to drop them off.

But before the divorce was finalized, there were those bittersweet moments when my daughters would come back from visiting their dad. They'd be full of stories about their adventures, excitedly recounting the fun they had. Yet, hidden among their joyful tales were the painful parts—the mentions of "Aunty so-and-so," who'd been around a lot. It didn't take long to realize that "Aunty" was their dad's new girlfriend.

I had this naive belief that even when couples are separated, they should wait until the divorce is final before starting new relationships. I thought it was an unspoken rule, a way to keep things less messy for everyone involved. But, apparently, I was wrong. People told me it's not even considered cheating because you're not living together anymore. A weird concept, right? But that's how it is.

For me, though, it felt like cheating, and it played a big role in my decision to push forward with the divorce. Jal seemed genuinely shocked when he realized I didn't know that being separated meant it was okay to find someone new. He looked at me with surprise, like, "How did you not know this?" And I just thought, "Seriously? Just like that?" It was a harsh reality to accept, but in the end, it only made me more certain that divorce was the right path for us.

Transitioning from separation to full-on single motherhood was like steering through a maze blindfolded. It's a role no one really prepares you for, a relentless rollercoaster of emotions and responsibilities. Yet, amid the chaos, there were moments of unexpected support and surprising gestures from my ex, Jal.

Sure, he wasn't around as much as before, but when the kids reached out with those burning questions or urgent needs, he was there, his voice on the other end of the line offering reassurance. His child support payments were consistent, arriving like clockwork every month. And beyond that, he'd go the extra mile, insisting I let him know if there was anything else they required. It was a generous offer, but it was one I hesitated to take up. Call it skepticism or pride, but I couldn't shake the feeling that nothing in life truly comes for free. So, I maintained my distance, allowing him to continue being the father they deserved while I played the part of the ever-resilient mom.

Instead, I nudged him to connect directly with the kids to figure out their needs firsthand. And to his credit, he always followed through. It was a relief for me, knowing that when he stepped in, I didn't have to dig deeper into my own pockets. "I'll manage," I'd tell him, brushing off his persistent offers of help. But Jal, he wouldn't let it rest. His insistence on providing for us, even after our marriage had crumbled, was both baffling and touching.

I dragged my feet, unwilling to plunge back into that administrative abyss. The paperwork loomed before me like a daunting mountain, another reminder of the pain and resentment that lingered from the end of our marriage. But Jal, relentless as ever, pushed me to take action, this time to file through the courts to have my child support payments increased. Jal would say, "I'm making more money now than I did during the divorce, which is what the current payment amount is based on, but the child support payments should be increased to match what I now make." He may have been the cause of some of my heartache, but his willingness to step up when it mattered most couldn't be denied.

So, with a heavy heart and a pen poised over the dotted lines, I filed those papers. Jal embraced the opportunity to make things right and to ease some of the burdens I carried as the primary caregiver. It was a gesture of kindness I hadn't expected, a glimmer of compassion amid the wreckage of our broken marriage. And for that, despite everything, I'm grateful.

Being a single parent isn't just a walk in the park; it's like juggling flaming torches while riding a unicycle on a tightrope. It requires a superhuman level of dedication, a bottomless well of love, and the wisdom to know when to lay down the law and when to let things slide. From ferrying them to music class to cheering them on at volleyball practice, the job description is as vast as the universe itself.

Sure, I get why some parents might be tempted to take the path of least resistance, to turn a blind eye when things get tough. It's tempting to think that letting things slide might be easier than putting in the hard yards. But trust me, that's a recipe for disaster. The key, I've found, is to put in the work now, to lay down those boundaries and instill those values while they're still young. Because when you strike that delicate balance between love and discipline, the payoff is immense.

And let's not forget the importance of faith. For me, it's been the bedrock upon which I've built my single-parent empire. Turning to a higher power, to His grace, has been my saving grace. It's what's kept me going when the going got tough, what's given me the strength to keep putting one foot in front of the other, even when it felt like I was wading through molasses.

And you know what? It's paid off in spades. Because despite the odds stacked against us, my kids have turned out to be nothing short of amazing. They're respectful, they're diligent with their studies, and they're racking up awards and accolades like it's nobody's business. From snagging the highest honors to representing their school at state board meetings, they're knocking it out of the park. And for that, I can't help but feel an overwhelming sense of gratitude. Thank you, universe. Thank you, God. You've turned what could have been a tragedy into a triumph.

Chapter Eight

Reconnecting with An Ex

The final act of my marriage to Jal felt like a Shakespearean tragedy – full of sound and fury, but ultimately signifying the end. We threw every ounce of effort into salvaging it, only to be met with the crushing truth: the curtain had fallen. The helplessness, the suffocating guilt of failing not just ourselves but our precious daughters – it was a weight that threatened to bury me. But even in the darkest moments, sometimes the only path forward is through. Divorce, as terrifying as it was, became our harsh reality.

Grief, however, was a luxury I couldn't afford. The cavernous emptiness left by the marriage's demise was quickly replaced by a fierce determination. My focus narrowed to a laser beam: shielding and empowering my girls. Dating was a distant melody in a land far, far away. New relationships would only introduce complications for which I just didn't have the bandwidth. And bitterness? Absolutely not. I nurtured a fragile bridge of communication with my exes, maintained a social life that revolved around park playdates and PTA meetings (hello, single mom life!), and refused to let the negativity take root.

Then, a glimmer of hope pierced through the storm clouds. Hanno, my ex-boyfriend from the previous chapter in my life, reappeared, this time holding the golden ticket – a dream job as his assistant at the UN. My heart soared – a chance to use my skills, to carve out a new path, to be a role model for my girls. But the euphoria quickly morphed into a tangled knot of worry. Who would watch the girls? Jal, of course, but that felt like a betrayal of their (and my) needs. Especially at this crucial age, they needed their mom, a constant presence, a steady hand to guide them through the ever-changing landscape of childhood.

Plus, there was the ever-present Jal-Hanno jealousy issue. Jal, bless his heart, was haunted by the suspicion that I'd eventually leave him for one of them (a notion so far from reality it was laughable!). This insecurity had been a persistent thorn in the side of our marriage, a constant battle I fought in vain. Trying to convince him to focus on the strength of our bond instead of the demons in his head… eventually ending our relationship. This job offer, as tempting as it was, presented a whole new set of hurdles, a complex equation with my daughters' well-being at its core. The decision loomed before me, a heavyweight in the palm of my hand.

Jal's ghost loomed large, and his accusations about Hanno constantly echoed in the back of my mind. Divorced, I was finally free to call the shots, yet his past insecurities felt like invisible chains binding me to a life I no longer desired. Respect was paramount to me, even for Jal, but this felt like a cruel balancing act.

The UN offer was a siren song, a promise of financial freedom, and a chance to carve my name into the world. It was everything I yearned for: a chance to be the strong, independent woman I knew I could be. But the potential consequences were a chilling symphony of doubts. Jal's inevitable heartache, the bewildered faces of my daughters – how could I justify leaving them behind, chasing a dream across an ocean? "Because money" wouldn't be enough. Not for them, not for the foundation I was desperately trying to build for our future.

Iraq itself presented another hurdle. As a woman of color, navigating a Muslim country would be a journey fraught with unknowns. Would my girls be ostracized, their innocence deemed a foreign concept? The image of them, lost and alone in a strange land, gnawed at my resolve. And who would care for them in my absence? The logistical nightmare, coupled with the emotional turmoil, was a tangled web I wasn't sure I could untangle.

The weight of these questions became an unbearable burden, a relentless tide threatening to pull me under. Accepting the job meant sacrificing precious pieces of myself, putting my daughters' well-being at risk. With a heart heavy, with a bittersweet mix of regret and relief, I declined Hanno's offer. He, to his credit, understood. Our friendship remained a lifeline, a shared history that transcended the miles. Jason, too, continued to be a confidante, a virtual shoulder to cry on through late-night texts. In the face of this agonizing decision, the support system I'd built, imperfect as it was, became a beacon of solace, a reminder that I wasn't alone in the storm.

Three years after the dust settled with Jal, fate (or maybe a rogue cupid with a mischievous streak) intervened. I met Somu, and things moved at warp speed. We were entangled in a whirlwind romance that fast-tracked itself straight into serious territory. Then, wham! Just as quickly as we fell for each other, I discovered I was pregnant.

Anger bubbled up inside me. Here I was, using a five-year birth control method – a way of my commitment to avoiding unplanned pregnancy, even when single. But life, it seemed, had a wicked sense of humor. My OB-GYN had advised a brief window without protection before a new insertion. It was during that narrow window, that cosmic joke of a timeframe, that I met Somu and – boom! – pregnant.

My mind was a whirlwind. Who was this guy I was building a life with at hyper-speed? A baby? What on earth was I thinking? Abortion, the logical solution, flickered in my head. Find a clinic, get it done, and problem solved. Yet, another voice whispered – the baby. What about the tiny life growing inside me? Who was I to play God? The answer, that elusive answer, remained frustratingly out of reach.

In the end, it was the baby, this innocent who hadn't asked for any of this, that swayed me. Fear of a higher power wasn't a factor – let's be honest, I wasn't exactly a saint. It was a decision made with a raw, primal instinct, a choice for this unknown future we were about to create together.

Somu was a walking contradiction. During the whole pregnancy drama, he never outright stopped me from getting an abortion, but his conflicted emotions hung heavy in the air. Relief washed over him when I decided to keep it, and from then on, he doted on the idea of becoming a dad. It was almost comical – this whirlwind romance that fast-tracked into an engagement with the plan of getting married in the future fueled by a surprise pregnancy.

Here's the kicker – Somu was a walking red flag disguised as a sex god. At first, his jealousy felt kind of sweet, a possessive intensity that fueled the passion like a shot of adrenaline. It made me feel desired, like a prize he was determined to keep. But the honeymoon phase wore thin faster than a silk scarf on a windy day.

The possessiveness morphed into emotional manipulation, a suffocating grip that felt less like a passionate embrace and more like a desperate attempt to control. He tried to mend his ways, poor guy, but the possessiveness was like a second skin he couldn't shed. Every conversation and every interaction felt like a tightrope walk, navigating a minefield of potential jealousy triggers.

But there was one undeniable perk to Somu – his skills in the bedroom were legendary. Let's just say intimacy was never a chore with him. He knew exactly how to push all the right buttons. Now, this is where things get interesting.

Culturally, I underwent female circumcision. It's a reality for many women, and reaching orgasm can be difficult, sometimes impossible. It's never bothered me – it's all I've ever known. But with Somu, orgasms were practically guaranteed, a demonstration of his impressive skills and a surprising twist in my own sexual history. Makes you wonder, right? I can't exactly compare my experience to others, but hey, no complaints here. In the land of the blind, the one-eyed man is king, as they say.

Somu might have been a jealous mess, but in that one arena, at least, he was a king.

Somu's jealousy reared its ugly head again, this time with a familiar face attached – Jal. Just like before, a shadow from the past loomed, twisting reality into a warped funhouse mirror. Somu was convinced Jal still held a torch, ready to snatch me away like a prize. Here I was, trying to build a future with Somu and our newborn son, only to be yanked back into the drama of my past. The irony was thick enough to spread – Jal had a new girlfriend, practically fiancée material!

For reasons that would soon become clear, this new woman decided friendship with me was in the cards. "Friends? Discussing Jal's…penis?" I scoffed. The idea was laughable. No sisterhood existed between us, not when she was clinging to a man who was clearly over me.

Then, the calls started. Every time my girls visited Jal, she would feel the need to update me on her "parenting skills" in a thinly veiled brag. "You're doing what you're supposed to do, lady; you're sleeping with their father; that's what you should do," I'd bite back, barely containing the frustration that bubbled within me. "Leave me alone!" This insecure shrew wouldn't take the hint.

The final straw came a day after giving birth to my son, Sonny E. Sandy-Jonjo Jr. (quite the mouthful, right?). July 9th - a day etched in my memory for all the wrong reasons. This woman called, oblivious to the state I was in. My body was still recovering from the monumental feat of childbirth, and frankly, I can't recall what nonsense spewed from her mouth.

But one thing was clear – the blood flow was heavier than usual, a terrifying consequence of childbirth. Tears streamed down my face as I pleaded for her to understand, to let a new mom rest. "You've been there, haven't you?" I choked out, referencing her own motherhood. Her response? A callous dismissal of my pain. Slamming the phone shut, I vowed to never pick up again.

Telling Somu was out of the question. More drama, more calls to Jal and his girlfriend – the thought was exhausting. So I kept it bottled up, the worry a heavy weight on my chest. Somu noticed the shift in my mood, but my lips remained sealed. The tears, though, flowed freely that night, soaking my pillow as I drifted into a troubled sleep. Exhaustion, physical and emotional, finally claimed me.

Eleven years later, the truth about that call exploded like a bomb. Jal confessed it was his state of pain that made his girlfriend call me. Apparently, Jal's pain over my having Somu's baby manifested in his sleep – sleep talking about me, no less! So his "girlfriend" took it upon herself to "help him out" by harassing me while I was literally hemorrhaging after childbirth. Fighting for her man? Or trying to assert dominance over a woman who'd clearly moved on? Either way, what a colossal lack of empathy! A brand-new mother, vulnerable and exhausted, was the target of her insecurity.

Fast forward, Somu and I did get engaged, and the whirlwind romance reached a (slightly premature) peak. But the drama, that ever-present shadow, loomed large. My patience, once elastic, finally snapped. The engagement was called off, leaving me a single mom to three brilliant, beautiful kids. It wasn't the easiest path, but hey, three strong personalities to raise keeps life interesting, to say the least.

Chapter Nine

Missed Opportunity

Jason and I had texted each other through Facebook over the years just to say hi and check up on each other, even while we were still married to other people. Jal knew about it and had always been okay with it. However, when I divorced Jal, he revealed that he had been really hurt by those interactions despite having given me permission. I was at a loss for words, genuinely sorry and saddened by his admission. I apologized to him, feeling the weight of his unexpected hurt.

After my divorce from Jal, I didn't inform Hanno or Jason right away. I needed time to figure out my life. On one particular day, Jason texted me, as we normally did every few years. Sometimes, it was two-year intervals; other times, it was three or four years. There was no specific timing. This time, his message coincided with a particularly difficult moment in my life—my father had just passed away. I informed Jason about my father's death, and he was deeply moved, having known my dad from back home. He inquired about the burial arrangements, the time of the burial, and other details. I explained that only the memorial service would be held in the United States but that my dad's remains would be taken back to Sierra Leone, West Africa, for burial.

Jason was incredibly supportive during this time, offering emotional support and showing genuine concern. I was thankful for his presence during such a difficult period. My dad's remains were flown back home and finally laid to rest in our village, next to his sister's grave, as he had wished.

During my conversations with Jason, I discovered that he, too, was now divorced. By the end of my dad's burial, we had rekindled our old friendship into a love relationship. He made me feel young and carefree again, a feeling I deeply cherished.

Jason visited me in Buffalo, New York, and old memories resurfaced, resurrecting feelings I thought were long gone. Later, we arranged for me to visit him in Maryland. As my birthday approached, he wanted us to celebrate it at his place in Maryland, and I accepted. He took care of everything, from purchasing my plane tickets to organizing the celebration with friends and family.

He went above and beyond to make my birthday special, and it truly was. Our first night together, and the ones that followed, were unforgettable. We shared gentle love-making, and his soft kisses on my forehead after each tender moment served as a confirmation of his affection and satisfaction. Our visits to each other became cherished and welcoming.

But then, the devil was never far away. On the day of my birthday, amidst the celebration, there she was—an obvious devil in our midst, one of his cousins named Dana, or as I came to think of her, the BITCH. From the moment I met her, I had a feeling something was not right.

She seemed to be sizing me up, and it became clear that she, along with Jason's mother, was still stuck on what Jason had gone through during his marriage and subsequent divorce. They were not ready to move on and were wary of anyone new in Jason's life. How was that fair, especially since I was a divorcee myself? But they couldn't see that, and their lack of understanding was disheartening. Despite the negativity, I tried to focus on the joy and love I had found with Jason, hoping that, in time, his family would come to accept and understand our relationship.

They didn't know what I had endured during my divorce or how I was striving to be brave and give love another chance. If only they knew. On the other hand, someone was trying to love unconditionally—your cousin or son, in the case of Jason's mother. Why would anyone want to undermine that? But this one cousin of his, Dana—DiDevil, that bitch—she was becoming a real pain. There were too many of them scattered all over the place. This particular bitch, known to have slept with one of her other cousins and recently abandoned by her husband for another woman, seemed to have a personal vendetta. I suspected she wanted Jason for herself; otherwise, why was she so involved and skeptical of me?

Dana pestered me with questions about Jal, asking all these stupid questions as if she were the one I was sleeping with. I didn't owe her any answers and refused to tolerate her nonsense. Unable to get to me directly, she devised a second strategy to undermine my relationship with Jason and his mother. She manipulated Jason's mother, Miss Clarina, who unfortunately succumbed to her influence. Before Dana's interference, it seemed Miss Clarina was somewhat accepting of me, though there were moments when I felt a frown forming on my face that I had to consciously ignore.

For example, when Jason wanted photos of us together, his mother never looked relaxed or smiled except when Jason was present. I discussed this with Jason, and he confirmed he had noticed it, too. To avoid further tension, I limited my interactions with her, but she must have noticed my avoidance because I began to feel unwelcome. I considered some of her reservations acceptable since she didn't know me—the woman who was going to be with her son, the woman her son loved so much even after all these years.

As a mother myself now, I knew I would never treat any potential or future sons- and daughters-in-law in a way that made them uncomfortable. I might have questions about my children's choices, but I wouldn't express them in a manner that made anyone feel unwelcome, at least not in their presence. That's not happening. Most importantly, I recognized that it wasn't my responsibility to choose my children's partners. That was too much work and one I wasn't willing to undertake.

Hence, with her limited love for her son, in my opinion, because if she really loved him and knew what her son had gone through, she should have done everything possible to be more understanding and tolerant in his interest, to say the least.

Things were building up inside me, even as I had other competing priorities in my personal life, such as being a student at the University at Buffalo and working on finishing my degree. I could only tolerate so much. When Jason informed me one day about a girl who needed help and a place to stay, he was getting too involved in the situation. He was coordinating between the girl's parents, involving other people who were reluctant to get involved, and the like. All these things were becoming too much for me to handle.

What I believe should have been done was for us to first discuss it and come up with a strategy to help her, such as locating an agency responsible for the homeless or even getting her an apartment. Instead, Jason and his mom decided on what to do without my input, and all he did was keep me updated. I could not accept that. I understand that people need help, but there's a way to go about it with respect. This person needed a place to live, but first, he should have involved his girlfriend from the start of these arrangements.

The final straw was when Jason informed me about the "homeless" girl who needed help. He got too involved in her situation. When Jason told me that he was going on a nine-hour drive to check on this "homeless" woman who was now hospitalized for a mental assessment, I knew I couldn't be part of it. Jason was not a doctor, nor was it an emergency that couldn't be discussed with me, his partner.

Then, the final blow came when Jason informed me that his mom was going to house her. What? She was going to do that without even showing some respect to me? Who did they think I was? Such disrespectful people. That, for me, was the final straw. I would not accept any form of disrespect.

So, I stayed away from all of them. I stopped taking Jason's calls and stopped calling his mom, and she did the same. I didn't respond to any of his texts anymore.

The fact is that Jason should have been able to act as he saw fit, but not while I still held the title of girlfriend. Also, I thought his mother knew very well that her son was in a relationship and should have considered that in her actions, but that wasn't the case. Such a mother and grandmother—this woman wouldn't allow her grandson to live or stay in her house, but she was willing to let a total stranger do so?

I couldn't fathom it, and I couldn't stand it. What the hell? Did she even love her son, the one who had been wanting me forever and now had the opportunity, only to have her undermine it? Poor Jason. She probably thought she was hurting me, but it had the opposite effect. I had to leave them alone before I said something I might regret.

Even as I protected my dignity and made a decision that demonstrated that a part of me, for some weird reason, felt badly and regretful for leaving Jason, I couldn't really say he intentionally tried to hurt me. I felt like he was in a place of vulnerability, especially after his divorce. I had experienced it myself; it felt like trying to reassure or prove to people that their approval mattered. One eventually gets out of it, but it takes time. For example, shortly after my separation and before the divorce was finalized, I enrolled in a community college with the plan to transfer to a university upon completing my associate degree.

During a conversation with someone I respected, she minimized my effort to attend a community college, saying, "…a community college?" with a negative connotation. That got to me. I didn't return to that college the next semester. Instead, I enrolled in a different college called ITT, which they approved. But that decision turned out to be wrong, and I'm still suffering from it 16 years later. Unlike the community college, which was accredited, ITT was not. I couldn't transfer the credits to any accredited university, and I still have the student loan attached to it.

Thinking about Jason, I realized he might be seeking approval and making poor decisions out of a sense of vulnerability. He wasn't intentionally trying to hurt me; he was just lost. However, I couldn't continue to be a part of a situation where I was disrespected and my feelings were disregarded. So, I stayed away from all of them, stopped taking Jason's calls, stopped calling his mom, and didn't respond to any of his texts anymore.

I guessed that Jason would eventually come out from under their spell, but only with time. They, too, would pay for their wickedness toward me. That woman, whose negative comment made me change schools, later attended the very community college she had criticized me for attending. Remember her? I didn't know why, but she must have paid for her wickedness; her husband divorced her, and the court awarded him custody of their children. I felt a little sad for her, especially for losing her kids—no mother should have to go through that. I might be biased, but I couldn't help it, being a mother myself.

Thinking back, I knew Dana's manipulative ways would eventually catch up with her. Her bitterness, fueled by her husband abandoning her, made her intent on spreading pain. And Miss Clarina, by causing Jason to lose the love of his life, might end up losing him forever. I hoped love would prevail in the end because love always wins, no matter what.

Chapter Ten

Uncertainty

Forget diamonds and riches; there's nothing quite like the intoxicating rush of love. It's the universal language, a melody sung by hearts overflowing with affection. Love comes in a million dazzling variations: the sweet and sassy banter of best friends, the fierce protectiveness of siblings, and the heart-stopping, butterflies-in-the-stomach kind that ignites between lovers. I, for one, feel incredibly lucky to have experienced most of this vibrant spectrum.

My love story began nestled in the warm embrace of family. My mom, a radiant sun in my childhood sky, showered me and my siblings with affection and attention – the whole shebang. These formative years painted a masterpiece of what love truly is for me. Here's the secret about love, the kind that truly endures: it's not about finding someone airbrushed with perfection; it's about finding someone kind enough to see the chipped paint and faded brushstrokes and love you fiercely anyway.

This philosophy became my personal compass, guiding me through life's uncharted territories and shaping how I navigate relationships. It's like having a built-in radar for disrespect – that grating sound throws the whole system off-kilter, prompting a reevaluation. With this love roadmap in hand, I've cultivated a deep sense of self-worth. I know I'm lovable, loving, and a whole constellation of other awesome things.

Maybe I could use a sprinkle of patience, though – especially for grown-ups who seem to have misplaced their maturity marbles. Seriously, universe, is there an app for that? Because watching adults throw tantrums is enough to make anyone yearn for a cosmic intervention.

There's also the ever-present quest for that special someone, the missing puzzle piece that completes the picture. Maybe they're out there, just waiting to be found, someone who shares this same understanding of love – the messy, beautiful, all-encompassing kind. Until then, I'll keep cherishing the love I already have, the love that continues to shape me, and the love that promises an exciting adventure for the heart.

Mom wasn't the only one who showered me with love. My dad was fantastic, too, but it's Granny Koteh, my amazing grandma, who holds a special place in my heart. Her laugh lines crinkled around her eyes, which always seemed to hold a twinkle, and her hugs were the warmest blanket on a cold night. (May her soul rest in peace). I miss her dearly. Then there's Uncle Foday, the one and only – though everyone else calls him Mr. Dumbuya. We all know it's the same phenomenal man! He treats us nieces and nephews like his own, a true blessing. I tell him I love him all the time, but maybe I need to bake him his favorite pie – actions do speak louder than words, right?

Now, my love life, haha? A bit of a mystery, much like a dusty antique shop waiting to be explored. A couple of days ago, a friend – a hilarious white lady, I might add – suggested, "Beatrice, let's find you a white guy!" We both laughed so hard we cried. "Maybe that's the answer!" I joked. But honestly, I'm not sure. Part of me wants to explore the unknown, a white guy perhaps, someone whose background adds a whole new layer to my love life. But then the familiar, the black guy territory, seems equally uncharted. (trails off, shrugs) Maybe the right guy isn't about race at all. Maybe he's around the corner, waiting to surprise me with a goofy grin and a heart as warm as Granny Koteh's pies. Who knows? Love is an adventure, and I'm ready for the ride.

Meanwhile, picture this: a friend with wanderlust in her eyes, hatching a plan for a road trip to Canada. Sounds epic, right? Except... I can't stand driving long distances. It's not the scenery; it's the endless hours trapped in a metal box hurtling down the highway that makes me fantasize about trading the steering wheel for a comfy hammock strung between two palm trees. So, I did what any reasonable person with a serious case of FOMO (fear of missing out) would do – I politely declined and then panicked because, well, a Canadian adventure still sounded pretty amazing.

Luckily, another friend, a total superstar with a heart of gold (and possibly a slight case of cabin fever – who wouldn't want to escape the US summer for a Canadian escape?), swooped in to save the day. This guy even braved the border crossing, all the way from Canada to the US, just to chauffeur us around. True hero status, unlocked.

Here's the twist (because life loves a good plot twist, doesn't it?): this same friend also happens to be my ex, Somu – the one who knows his way around, remember? (Wink, wink). Now, you might think being stuck in a car with your ex for a weekend could be a recipe for disaster, especially when he clearly wants to rekindle things. And let's be honest, being single has its downsides. But my family, bless their hearts, is like a well-meaning but slightly overbearing Greek chorus in a modern-day rom-com. They hold onto the past tighter than I hold onto a good cup of coffee, and the pressure to "Not give him another chance" was real. Talk about a test of my resolve!

Canada was a blast, by the way. Breathtaking scenery, delicious poutine (because what's a Canadian adventure without poutine?), and enough laughs to make my cheeks hurt. But the real adventure was navigating the emotional rollercoaster of being stuck in close quarters with an ex and the ever-present pressure from my family. Let's just say it was a Canadian adventure I won't soon forget.

We all like to think we're Captain Kirk, boldly charting our own course through the galaxy of life. But truth be told, sometimes the asteroid belt of family advice can throw us way off course.

Here's the deal: My ex, Somu, saw our Canadian adventure as a chance to rekindle the flame. Let's just say the embers were pretty cold on my end. But my ever-vocal family started whispering about another ex who was also vying for my attention. One might think, with two exes vying for a shot, this is a dream come true. But nope, more like a romantic traffic jam.

Suddenly, I'm stuck in a love triangle. Do I follow the familiar path with Somu, the one who aced the hero test by chauffeuring us across the border? Or do I explore the unknown with the other ex, a potential adventure waiting to unfold? Maybe there's a whole new love waiting around the corner, a love that hasn't even shown its face yet, a love that would blow both these exes out of the water.

The truth is, I have no freaking clue. But hey, that's the beauty of life, right? It's one giant, messy, unpredictable adventure. And even though I might need a celestial pit crew (looking at you, universe) to change my flat tire every now and then, I'm strapping myself in and holding on for the ride. Because who knows? Maybe this next adventure will lead me to the love story I've been waiting for, a story filled with fireworks, not awkward exes and whispered family ultimatums. Wish me luck! In the meantime, maybe I'll write a strongly worded email to my family, politely requesting they take a vacation from my love life.